BURDEN OF LOVE

POEMS

**WRITTEN
BY**

LAVI PICU

BURDEN OF LOVE

Text Copyright © 2017 by Lavi Picu.

ALL RIGHTS RESERVED

Publication date: 2017-11-01
Printed and Bound within USA.

First edition First printing

ISBN:
EBook: 978-0-9959589-3-7
Paperback: 978-0-9959589-2-0

ĐEDICATION

To Julie, my muse, who never let the ink dry.

To my mother, who always believed in happy endings.

*To all those who shaped me by showing me
the wide array of shades of love.*

*To all women who want and deserve to be loved
properly.*

To all of you, who still believe in Love.

TABLE OF THOUGHTS

TABLE OF THOUGHTS

TABLE OF THOUGHTS

It's a long read, so grab a nice warm cup

of tea, relax and enjoy the experience!

8

A LONELY VIOLIN

The Dogons witnessed in slow motion the birth of clouds,
taking with them the secrets of the invisible world,
leaving behind songs and chants, old as the centuries,
formulas of potions altering states, unspoken languages
and lotus flowers to remind us of their wisdom.

Glimpses of casted shadows dance on the walls
while outside, the rain vanishes, bursts into smaller drops
leaving the sacred matriarch baffled, unaware of the
outcome, racing to the source, hoping the invisible war could
be won.

The gold age is starting now, the resistance has flatten;
bugs and birds lurch through the air, competing for sunlight.

1

The chain is pulled... we are running out of time,
we can't see it, as we are so absorbed;
we're slow and weak, although we think invincible.

The bubble's power creates new streams of wave
energy,
its speed fires up seeds in all directions,
sending them far enough to avoid competition.

All you can hear is an old chant, a lonely violin.

A PLACE I LONG TO BE

There's a place I long to be where
my heart's free of misery,
I don't have to sleep alone,
my soul finds salvation,
my curves meet adoration.

There's a place I long to be
and get rid of all this insanity
where I could be myself again
where I pray to return and stay
forever lost and abandoned into your arms.

There's a place I long to be
for a thousands reasons more,
where all regrets or fears vanish
where the dawn of day brings
only love and serendipity.

I know the way that leads me there:
 one way ticket to ride
the tidal wave that rises ahead of me
washing up all that I've known before you,
flattening wishes and beds, words, eyes and threats.

A POEM'S BIRTH

Grab the shovel,
drop the gravel-
it's time to lay it all out;
bring a bottle,
wipe your sweat,
let's make this baby
sprawl, roll a cigarette.
Your wits and the pen
in my hand make us a band,
will scribble till dawn,
pour magic in all,
words will fight facts,
knights will bow their hats
unburying their lost faith...

AGAIN

Eyes wide open,
I am walking on my toes,
trying to gain some
balance.

Wheels are rolling,
still on the first gear...
did I vanquish
my fear?

Restrained by my own common sense,
dazzled by the freedom-flow,
I let the actor play
the part.

Arms crossed on my chest,
I walk around, alone,
sunburnt,
again.

Five thoughts fly me somewhere else,
rescued by a sparkling anchor,
my humour drifts far,
far away.

ANCHORED

Each time I close my eyes to blink
I feel the burden of that second
cause I'm afraid to lose the sight of you,
that I'll no longer breath your air
nor touch your skin or kiss those lips-
who weren't mine to kiss at all,
within this lifetime when you're anchored.

To be truthful, they were mine, I had them first,
but unfortunately for a while I lost their trace,
their precious smile disappeared from my face,
all I remembered was their shape and thirst.

I know for sure that we're meant to be,
you talk to me about God and poetry
leaving behind my humble misery.

I dare to dream of better, longer days and tenderness,
with chocolate for breakfast, whispers and caresses,
though for the moment I live and feed on memories
of purple walls, wet sheets, coffee and old stories.

BREAKOUT POINT

Felt so betrayed for living in a lie
you've nurtured at your best;
years ago, you'd thought you'd die,
an anger roar swam through your chest.
You tripped and fell on your illusions,
it hurt a lot! There were no cushions!
Don`t you think it`s kind of stupid
at your age, to still believe in Cupid?
Put all the plans out on the board, say it loud:
"*I got stronger, time to move on!*"
Patch all your dreams, and cry no longer.
Damn! Who unplugged the cord?
Starting today, you don`t remember
where were you or who was Amber!

BROKEN SOUL

If I only could turn into your shadow
maybe then I would stop missing you,
I'd be able to fly with you everywhere
I'd be with you, follow you silently.

I would not mind you stepping over me,
I'd embrace the shape of your feet
leaving a sweet kiss upon their soles
to make you feel loved once more.

The sun and the moon would be my only chance
to reach the clouds and leave the Earth behind,
I have been waiting for a sign for so long...

I've been hoping to get away from this ocean of looks,
to reach that lost dream of burning hearts and
whispers, melted by the early dawn,
in sweet slumber's embrace.

I am struggling to find the spark that kept us alive,
I remember its echo, it sounds like a refrain -
in my mind, it has been playing on and on;
blindfolded I walk on, looking for its source.

Please let me feel what you feel,
bring out all what you have been hiding,
I want to know it all; your secrets,
fears and sins can't be worse than mine!

Turn me on with your eyes,
let me rise with you,
help me find the love
once more before it dies.

I want to hear each single thought
running through your head:
unravel the burden, let the rain melt
and drain what the heart ached or fought.

Bend and curve the lines of our twisted faith,
stop worrying and seeing everything in grey,
hold my hand and walk with me on this path,
leave your fears behind, we'll find our own way.

Try to remember the promises we made,
whatever was not said, can make the hope die;
chase away the silence, ask me anything,
wash away the pain from my eyes and soul.

Throw your arms around me,
squeeze me without saying a word,
let me have my last breath there,
fly towards the sunset with me,
chasing a kite or a white cloud...

I am a passenger within this life,
each day starts with you,
each night ends with me,
the clouds are bringing the storm...

I am a dreamer completely lost
within the sweetness of this embrace,
where flesh and shadow touch fingers
and toes, where I am forever yours.

BURDEN OF LOVE

I walk through darkness
breathing out love,
the souls I met on the way
they all bow and make way.

Aimlessly swimming into this sea of grey,
carrying the burden of love which
lightens up with each step
I take closer to home.

Embraces, kisses and sweet memories
rewind in my mind as I pass
long forgotten lands where
humankind lost battles and hearts.

The gardens I crossed were all
welled by the tears and fears
I have left behind,
escaping the world's biggest sickness:
        "the *Expectation*."

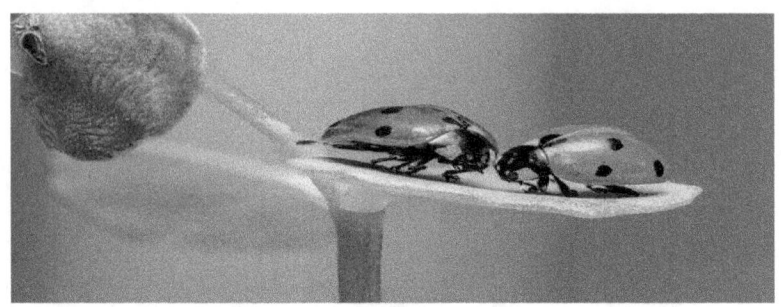

BURNING TEARS

All my dreams swim within a sea of grey,
struggling to survive to find the shore;
their tears ran dry and they wonder how
they can't understand why
love keeps two hearts apart.

One dream who missed you, tried to trick the time
and flew away, hungry to hear your breath...
Even the dreams dream to have a day
where they all will come true;
no one has the answers,
I feel their burning tears
coming down on me.

CHANGE YOURSELF!

Change yourself, change your fortunes!
you owe it to yourself to do it, until it`s too late!
When you least expect it, Life sets you a challenge
just to test your courage and willingness to change.

At such a moment, there is no point in pretending
 that nothing has happened, saying you're not ready;
the challenge will not wait, Life does not look back.
A glance is more than enough to decide whether or
not you accept your role, shaking hands with destiny.

Pitiful is the person who is afraid of taking risks,
I lost my fear of being disappointed or disillusioned-
suffering, I got good at this game.
I know I will fall on the way, but I follow my dream!

I won't look back to hear the whispers of my past
I look forward, I'm anchored in my future,
where I know I'll be who I need to be.
This time, I will, I will listen to my heart.

CHANGING SKIES

Wake up and look at the sky,
put yourself together,
aim your dreams high
and make it all the way
while you're still alive.

Here, there, everywhere,
time is everything -
I don`t wanna waste it anymore
gonna make the future mine.

Life is a beautiful mess,
it ain't a game of chess,
it`s about emotions and
words we use recklessly.

We waste priceless moments
which will never come back,
so end this foolish act,
be aware of contradictions
and see where we are.

CHECK OUT POINT
(LOVEY DOVEY)

When you reached the check out point
and everything is left behind,
no faults, wonders, doubts or what ifs,
you gave up glamour, thrills and butterflies,
you lost fear, shadows and regrets,
cause somewhere on your twisted path,
long time ago, you learnt the hard way
that the right choice was less
than you'd regularly settle for
and still that little meant the world to you,
when you tucked your demons into bed
and solved all the pieces of the puzzle,
then you could say you loved,
my lovey dovey buff.

CHOCOLATE

I know this chocolate woman
I've seen her on my way,
almost each day
we rode the bus together.

Still hope my mood gets better...
She had a jasmine scent,
turned heads while she bent
with her jeans, the latest trend.

She wore her dark hair up
always had some make-up
doing the last touch up
before the bus stopped.

She leaned on the window
her forehead bent,
squinting the horizon
trying to find a hint of her next vent...

*

I'm scribbling in here,
my words make no sense,
the meaning is lost; so is my youth,
but I don't regret trading it for the vermouth.

COLEEN - "DA BIN"

It`s surprisingly quiet...
girl, switch to a different diet!
I lost track of time...
I`m tired to see you`re sweet as a lime!
It`s been a while,
and you`re still on denial...
You give me no choice,
I`d do anything, but listen to your voice!
You must be a fan of the hard core,
cause you keep asking for more.
You've been haunting my mornings,
ignored all the warnings,
hovering over my head...
Why don`t you resign instead?

CONFESSION OF A LITTLE GIRL

I confessed my love to you lately -
I tried to do it more often and openly
when I realized time worked against me.

Each step forward for me
means one backward for you;
each year brings me
closer to my dreams and
gets you closer to your death.

How can I be happy
when I know this means
a closed road for you,
a dead end for both of us...

25

DADDY

Daddy never taught me how to dance
he preached moral, rules,
God, religion and common sense.
Daddy never warned me about you
being sick and slicker than the flu!
Who knew the devil was you?
Daddy preached about things
I couldn't see nor reach...
He saved souls from being doomed
helped the missies getting pruned
eased couples getting groomed.
Daddy taught me devil's around,
sex mainly was its playground,
waiting for us to sin and spoon
early mornings and late afternoons.
Daddy never taught me how to dance...

DID YOU?

Did you ever wonder
what keeps you still going
or what makes the difference between the days?
Why do the small little things make you smile?
Would you call that happiness?

Who connects the dots in your life?
Is it all caught in the net?
Who did you leave outside?
Who did you let in?

What is your gift? Did you ever use it?
How well you master it?
Where did your past lead you?
What was the lesson you learnt?

Did you notice everything goes in circles?
-goes around, comes around -
same script, new actors...
Do you alternate the parts?

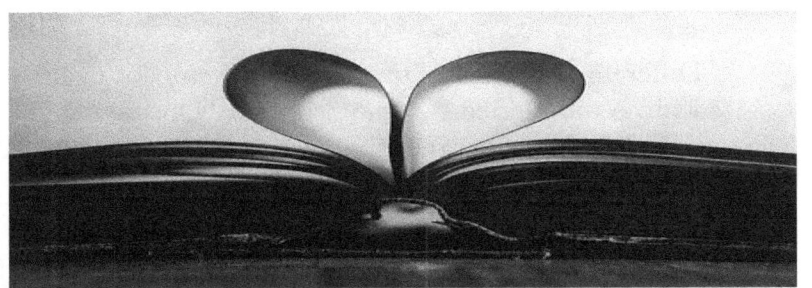

DIFFERENT

I left my all at your feet: my clothes, my love, my
shame, my sins, my everything;
I came to you barefoot and dropped the pile of things,
sins and hearts I walked on.

You asked me if the thorns made my soles bleed and
took my feet into your care, to help the healing,
without prying into the paths they've walked,
crawled or ran on.

Different, that's the word I'd use to describe
the feeling that started to warm up my soul;
everything you ever said, did or taught to me was
different.

29

Different than the rest of men that I've met or dealt with. A mesmerizing *different*, effortlessly luring me in, until I've fallen for you, without having a chance to understand what really happened.

No questions asked, no time to argue, the rule was clear: giving you back without shedding a single tear. A sad sweet kiss and your two hands around my face, is what I last remember -it broke my heart in two.

Will there be another moment in time for us to meet and love again? The journey never ended, it may have had a detour or a dry loop, but that's all -its end is far from near!

So far I witnessed this love's seed sprawl into a shear thunderstorm, spawning twisters and bringing hails, just to see it trifle away in the fall. The storm has passed but you're still here, trapped and buried deep within my soul.

How could I ever think that I'd be strong enough to cross or trot the world alone, without having you as my guide, by my side,

teaching me about the unseen worlds, telling me
stories of ancient cultures and their wise Gods,
helping me grow?

Sometimes I think that if we'd ever had a fight, then I
could gain harmony again...
I could hang on for a while to that bitter side of me,
hoping that its sad refrain
 would make me find an easier way to deal with the
pain of not having you here,
thinking that maybe hating you would sweeten the
deal and I'll live without fear.

DREAM SELLER

I told you about my maple leaf pink dream,
you bought it and followed the stream;
I wanted you to feel like home
you transformed it in a dome.

I showed you the world around
but you chose to see only the background,
ignoring the fact the life was made out of
small little unique moments of love.

I shared my dreams with you and hoped
that for once you'd let your ego go
and enjoy the feeling of freedom,
 have fun and just go with the flow.

I sold my dreams and paid the bills
trying to smooth the things and push forward;
between your constant wants and wails,
I stood no chance! I couldn't take it anymore...

DREAMING

"I dreamt a butterfly
Or did he dream about me?"
Memories emerged within a dream
which`s script you couldn't edit
or forge during the years,
awakening the monsters
you'd striven to burry deep,
to save your tears.

She was only a child, about four years old,
with no parental comfort, feeling cold.
No one to take her side, or think
she`d be in actual danger
while sent to spend the day away,
be treated as a stranger.

The neighbour, an old rotten wretched soul,
laid his eyes on you, watched her crawl,
pushed your stroller, made you smile,
kindly asked you, after a while,
if you'd need an extra hand,
giving you no time to comprehend
his real intentions.

DRUNK ALLEY CAT

Wake up! Wake up! It's time to party!
Wake up! Arch your back and let's be wild!

I'm nothing like an ordinary cat,
don't ask me about whereabouts',
the collar or my pedigree,
I eat, play, sleep, chase mice,
I play, all this cause I'm free.

No owner or master to overfeed me or spoil me
rotten,
no hands to brush, wash or tickle my belly buttons,
no mood swings that I have to endure,
no funny dresses, or silly diapers to wear,
no forced training for the litter box.

I have no stress,
I live free because
I'm proud to be
a drunken alley cat.

EMPTINESS

When there's no substance, no content
and you're starring at this empty sheet
with nothing to say or scribble,
you'd better leave it all blank!

Look around and choose your words,
don't blame me for your discontent,
unravel your burden without shame,
let your heart whisper its stories.

That emptiness within your heart
needs to be filled with something else
than hate, sorrow and pain. Hope!
Hope for a better happy ending!

ENOUGH IS ENOUGH!

Where do I find the patience to remain silent or
what could give me the strength of bearing more
when the simple sound of your voice is unleashing
a long forgotten anger and resentments?

Being away for so long, out of your reach,
I forgot that within your presence I should
keep my demons tamed. How could I
have been so foolish to think you'd behave?

You say you care and do your best to help others
-though your victims have witnessed your act
at first hand – they would tend to say otherwise...
All that I care for, is to know that you're fine and alive.

39

For what is worth, I've left behind those times, unlike you, I moved forward. So should you! There is no point living in the past, dwelling in the pain, never letting your scars heal.

   Just let go!

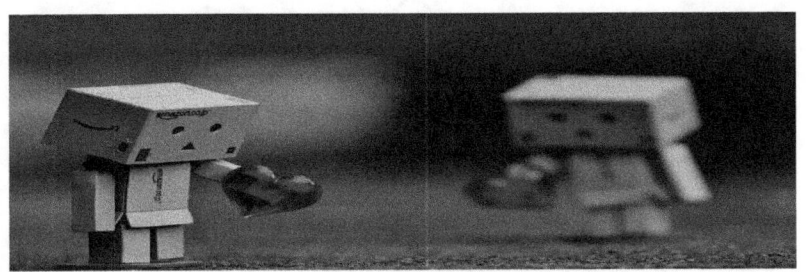

FAREWELL MY BITTER GIRL!

You turned sixteen and left the nest,
walked out the door and hoped for the best,
embraced new ways, fought violent gusts
just to prove a point, to live without "*musts*".

"*See you at the bitter end*!" was your last remark;
you were just sixteen when you hit the road
and vowed out loud to never come back,
rebelled against most of the rules, have to-s, musts.

Your thirst for knowledge lead your path
fuelled your quest and raised some doubts,
it took you places, continents, it showed you worlds
you'd never seen nor dreamt that they existed.

You've been searching for your Graal
around the world for quite some time...
towards the end you realized
that the battle you've looking for
was already taking place somewhere else,
somewhere you'd never thought of looking:
deep down inside you, where it all began and ended!

> *Before I take another step,*
> *we need to talk. Things have changed.*
> *Now I have found my peace,*
> *and I'm moving forward -though,*
> *I need you to grant me a favour:*
> *it's time to let go all the anger!*
> *Farewell, my bitter girl!*

FEARING DEATH

Although I'm far away from you,
I kept you hidden in my heart for so long
that I even forgot you were there.

I told myself too many times you were to blame
but in the end, I realized the problem wasn't you,
nor the blame, or pain, but the fear of loosing you.

Unwilling to leave room for this to happen,
I tried to make the fear go away
by using different tricks and poisons.

How could I ever be ready to lose you?
It's a selfish act, I know! I can't do it!
I don't think I'll ever be prepared!

Only the thought of this dark perspective
squeezes my chest as a constrictor,
springing rivers of tears and endless fears
of years in pain, without you.

The selfishness, guilt and fear prevented me
for spending more time with you
to get to know the person who you really are,
not the one I thought you were;

to let you see who I am from head to toe,
to share with you my pains and sorrow;
maybe I shouldn't have posed as brave and strong,
and I should have asked for your help.

FOOL' S GOLD

My quest for love and happiness lead me
on different continents, where I've dug
for gold and silver for a while.
I thought that I could replace the beauty
of a feeling with the sparkling metal;
I lost myself within the world for a few years.

When I finally came back to my senses,
I understood that I had taken a wrong path
which made dove right on the bottom of the
biggest open-pit.
That free fall woke me up and made me see
I was mining my chances, wasting my resources
on fool's gold. Bottom line: It was time to go!

I had been living somebody else's life for so long,
and I needed to start the re-genesis process;
kept only a nomad soul, forgot all about the gold,
picked the closest road and roamed,
escaping the daily routine and endless worries,
having the road as my friend and reward.

FREEDOM

I lived among the dead until I found no reason to stay,
with no one to care my hurt or my heart,
I broke my chains and walked away
I set myself free...

Free from all the non-sense agony I have lived in;
I had to hold it all together, had to be strong,
life and death hit me out of nowhere,
barely holding on, still... I moved on.

I closed my eyes and let it go;
it was hard to lose control,
though once I did, the game has changed-
I found sweet freedom in surrender,
though didn't turn me into His defender!

I started having brighter days,
almost forgot my darker pains,
morning tamed my older demons,
rescued what was left of me...

I learnt where to find my rest,
lay me head upon his chest,
save my tears for something
that's really worth...

GREEN EYES

Friday came and green candles burned,
throughout the day I lit them all,
thinking it might help you find your way back,
worried Morpheus might fall for those green eyes
I always cherished....

I feared he may want to prolong
their delightful spark within his kingdom.

Hours went by, one after another,
the deafening silence fed my anxiety,
a thousand thoughts of you
with different outcomes ran through my head...

I chased away all dreadful,
harrowing ones by saying one more prayer.

Stared at some of your old photos,
remembering long summer walks,
wondering wherever the steps
will take us both on this path we share
while you were fast asleep by pain
and the morphine was taking over.

HAPPINESS THAT'S A NEW THING

Happiness, that's a new thing...
maybe not to you, but it is to me-
hope it isn't just a fling
and it's here to stay.

At last, I got a taste of it,
after nightmares and despair,
after herxes, pains and flares,
I learnt its sweet perfume.

Smiling faces, pastel colours,
inner strength reveals itself;
season dies, I get my wings...
happiness is the new thing!

Spiders, pumpkins, spooky whispers
can't inspire more fear or distrust,
now I look around with calm,
knowing it's not witchcraft.

HEAVEN'S GUEST

I traded suits throughout my life,
I enjoyed trinkets, drinks and rolls of smoke,
laughing out loud at those who called me sinner
or tried to sway my beliefs regarding the black cloak.

Unwilling to suffer within my time
I didn't care not even for a second
that I was tarnishing my soul...
Oh, my love was so so small!

It didn't know the greatness of pure love,
I hadn't witnessed the heaven's glow
nor worried about the hollowed depths below,
whatever came my way, I dove.

While laying down on my death bed
I felt the heat approaching,
I saw those creepy eyes tinted red,
who ordered me to leave,
lifting me up without a gesture
dragging me down, taking me away.

They showed me depths and fire pits
I've never seen or heard of, unknown to man,
they made me walk a path of burning spears;
it spooked me out, letting out all of my fears.

When asked to leave the path and take a leap,
I looked up and allowed my grain of faith
to remember a long forgotten prayer
my father used to say to me at night.

Stiff and darkened within a glance,
with nothing but my pile of sins as burden,
I reached the judgement chamber
where time stood still and air whispered my sins.
I changed the stiff charcoal suit to sparkling glass,
witnessed the balance going down, then going up

until I reached the light and found the gate to heaven;
unworthy to step in, I stopped and awed in
contemplation.

Somehow there was no matter to step on,
everything seemed to be floating on thin air
as if we're in a different dimension, a new realm,
where I was given a guest's shiny suit
which made me see an endless place of love...

Remember:
A devil's prayer is the curse!

Words couldn't ever describe the beatitude of heaven,
its brightness, beauty, peace or its glory...

I've seen a different world, though not with these eyes,
I have heard voices, though not with these ears,
I talked and spoke, though not with this mouth
I walked but not using my feet,
I was a guest in heaven!

HOPE FOR SOMETHING BETTER

Autumn is here, take care of my heart,
cover it gently with a soft blanket
of warm kisses and tender caresses,
lay around it a bed of whispers
to snug in for the winter to come.

My worn soul can't find its sleep -
it wonders away through the world
ailing those in need, healing old
wounds and nestling hope
for something better.

The thoughts I had were blown away,
the words I had prepared, all failed to say
loneliness was what I feared the most,
being alone, without you...

HOW MUCH YOU LOVE ME

My darling, you say you love me and adore me,
though your hands touch other hands,
your eyes meet different other eyes
in the morning light on the bed sheets.

You say we've been soul mates for more than ten lives
that within this one, we are also meant to be together,
that we are wired by invisible ties and memories,
where we found and lost each other on and on.

Who invented this game of keeping hearts apart,
when we all wanted to see our dreams come true?
I am afraid of losing this game, the stakes are too high
I wish things were different and I wouldn't have to
miss you so much...

Maybe I am asking too much, but I am fighting time
I lost more than two decades, I have to make up for it
I'd trade anything to go back in time, change paths,
just to have you beside me, whispering me
how much you love me...

I no longer wish to live between two worlds
might be hard to believe but I want to settle down;
tell me my love, are you ready for such commitment?
You feel in love, but you have no clue that it comes
with a price...

I AM ALIVE

Cars can be fixed,
clothes can be stitched or sewed,
flowers can be grown and replaced
but people can`t be fixed,
and souls can`t be patched...

When I feel the pain,
instead of crying,
I tell myself that
      I AM ALIVE!

For that I am grateful,
and because of it,
I'll fight with all my strength
to see another sunrise
and sleep when the sun goes to bed.

After the crawlers made their claim,
and the twitches and burning have
finished their reign, I will find my peace.

Until then,
      I AM ALIVE!

I WANT STATEMENT

I WANT
a new job, a new boss, a new challenge,
a new start, a new life,
a new flat, a new country.

I WANT
new people, new friends,
quiet nights and sweet mornings.

I WANT
to write and read,
get published
and reviewed.

I WANT
to paint and play with colours,
to feel free of fears,
to share no more tears.

I WANT
to discover new worlds,
understand others better,
get enlightened and fly.

I WANT
to have time
to enjoy my life and LOVE.

I WANT
to see you get better,
relieved of pains.

I WANT
to grow up
and old with you.

I WANT
to see the sunrise
without sleepy eyes.

I WANT
to have dark chocolate,
calories free.

I WANT
to feel young
even in my 70's.

I WANT
to learn more,
new customs,
signs and languages.

I WANT
to have and raise a child,
and leave a mark behind.

I WANT
wisdom and serendipity
as my legacy.

I WANT
to change
somebody`s life
by being an inspiration.

I WANT
to keep alive all friends
throughout my life.

I WANT
to miss long winter nights
and snow throughout
an endless summer.

I WANT
to teach my kid
what values are.

I WANT
to reinvent myself
and amaze you more and more.

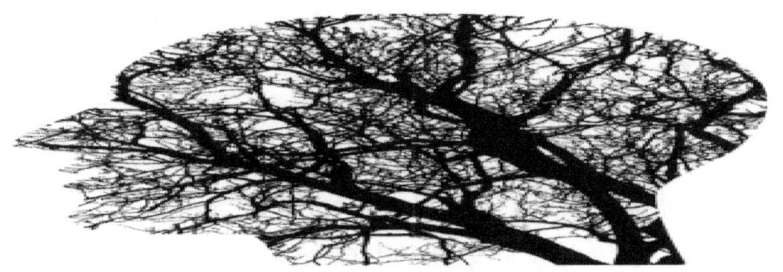

JEALOUSY

Only a fool could believe
there`s a cure for jealousy!
Don't you know that the heart
has its own way of dealing with
unfaithful treacherous thoughts?

Here you are, killing time on the net
chatting with some anonymous writers
hoping you'd get some answers to
the questions and doubts seeded
in your mind by the fear of being alone.

What do you think you'd achieve
by pouring out venom and opening wounds
we sunk deep in a drawer and we thought forgotten?

Consumed by inner fears
you seem to neglect that,
nothing happens under the sun
without a reason, without consent
or the will to forgive and forget.

LAST WAKE UP CALL

Time to break out from your cocoon,
time to leave aside fear and pain,
time to stop being your first enemy,
time to say things straight,
time to end an illusion,
time to kill the delusion.

Leave no space for any confusion
....with or without you...
time to spring out and breath in,
time to regain control,
time to squash the resistance
to its last reminiscence.
Wake up little girl and pack again,
the time is up- this window is closing!

LETTER TO DAD

Maybe I asked too much or
it was awry being away,
assuming you were fine.
I was wrong to believe
that we'd never change
that you're doing fine,
living in your world,
never understanding mine,
being always self occupied,
hiding behind excuses and
comfortably buying out my guilt.
I am not mourning,
cause you're still alive;
I hope and pray you'd be around
for many many more years.

It's a paradox- our fights and arguments
were always about God's existence-
and in the end, I pray to Him:
for your life, health and well being.

How could I have been so reckless
to waist not one or two,
but twenty years on playing silly games?

I close my eyes and I see us dancing
hands in hands, on a Cantata of Bach,
me imitating a soprano and you,
my partner, playing a conductor...

Those days when we're listening
to your mag were fabulous;
the memory still gives me the
shivers and goose bumps -
if I could only turn back time...

What I never told you nor confessed
was the impact you had on my upcoming,
 the way you touched my soul,
my heart, my youth, my whole life.

Everything was shaped by values
you preached and thought me;
I doubt there was a moment when
I wasn't proud of being your daughter.

LATE DECEMBER THOUGHT

Since I can`t go blank as you do,
I leave my mind err with no specific target,
hoping to leave the day behind.

I see bits of the past and
sparks of an alternative future-
feels like a déjà-vu...

Can`t tell for sure if
it`s a better one or not,
I guess I`m happy with my choices.

My legs are tired and my tights are hurting,
same old pain takes over again;
numb and all alone I dream of
white sands and the jade sea- my only refuge...

71

I fall asleep listening to the waves
I go back in time and take a different turn,
just to make sure I'll never meet
the one who`d become the clown.

But though, if I`d never met him,
probably I`d never met you too.
And if I`d had never met you,
I would not have been so foolish
to believe in that time-window theory.

Then I would have lived a perfect life -
deluding myself;
that joke could have ended
worst than it already did...

How bad do I really wish to have met you?
Well, don`t need to answer this. You know it!
Whispers fade out slowly, no more questions...

LIGHT UP THE NIGHT!

Light up the night,
aim your dreams high,
no matter if you fail
allow yourself to fall!

Next time you'd land better
don't wait until you're told
that it's your turn to shine!
Get out, work hard, be ready!

You owe it to yourself,
never give up the fight,
you have only one life,
once chance to burn that light
before this chapter's closing!

LOVE IS NOT ENOUGH

What do you do when you are all out of love,
searching the passion which made you dove,
when even your inner tears are all dried up,
and everything turned into daily routine,
chatting about meals and what is to clean?

I say: "*I miss you!*", you miss the city,
I say: " I *love you!*", you use it with scarcity,
I wanna kiss in public, you become phobic,
I dream having kids, you avoid such topics.

Everything turns to be upside down and
you wonder whose dream is this in the end.
How do you cope with the feeling of guilt,
is there anything left from the dream we built?

How can you tell words you do not feel
we are falling apart, each one playing a different act
in this play; I guess we all forgot
how it felt to be loved, alive.

Please tell me what to expect from all this
when you cant remember the day we first kissed;
five years passed since we started it together,
genuinely we thought it would last forever,
both thinking that love is more than enough
to keep us going together on the same path.

MY SILENT ROAR

I wrote a line and hit delete
thinking that you won't get
what I was trying to say...
I tried once more to convey
my misery but I got to a point
where I hit the wall.

I felt so weak as if I had no strength,
like I was facing a dead end.
I could not find my words and say
I wanted you close, not far away,
I was tired of us living this way,
my heart and soul were falling apart.

76

From all the days that passed, today,
I needed you to be here, the most.
I longed to hear your voice, to lift me up,
to tell me that we'd be ok, to hold me tight
and say that you shared my pain, to wipe
my tears and promise that it won't happen
again, to help me from drowning in despair.

I set a new record for my lowest low,
I did not know love equalled pain;
I am sailing on a sea of grey
drifting away to uncharted waters
hoping that somehow the compass
will light my way to you again.

I tried to see the brightness in despair,
to look for hope while bidding "*Adieu*"" to the deaths;
I cried and mourned my loss, all alone in silence,
calling out your name, hoping you'd hear
my silent roar and chose to let your anchor go,
rushing to set sail towards me.

MOOSE

We claimed this land as ours,
we cut a road throughout the middle,
and advertised its presence, the mighty moose,
by drawing it on huge green boards,
we've seen so often on the roadside.

We took a mental note,
drove on, enchanted by the landscape,
never thought we`d get so *"friendly"*
nor imagined that the "wild life"
would be landing on our windshield.

Being alive today, I`d call it simply *"miracle"*
-played on, and on, the scene within my mind,
tried to dilate the time, to cover every angle,
in order to explain "*the bond*" created within seconds.

Under the rain of shattered glass
a scream of fear awakened the whole forest,
eyes closed, I turned my back
and sought for refuge.

ON MY WAY

On the path called LIFE
I am pursuing my quest.

I have been wandering
for almost two decades,

being a digital nomad
for the last ten years.

Sometimes, the loneliness
made me forget what was I looking for;
I spent some time here and there.

I met new people, and
when I started to feel attached,
I hit the road again.

I`m like the gypsies,
always on the road,
always ready to leave.

Couple of times,
I lost the path and
almost gave it up;

I even dared my faith
and took an oath.

That was the first mistake!

ONCE UPON A TIME

"Once upon a time..."- that's how it all starts...
with hopes and dreams, laughter or tears,
snare drums, dazzling lights, sips of sweet wines
on a rooftop kissing the breeze, simple summer tease.

A dare to see what hides beneath some dark eyes,
an ear to hear some old untold vows to be vowed
of the years that passed -the main chip collapsed;
back in the game -sobriety yet to be attained,
knees to be bent and drinks to attend.

Nothing on display, focused on foreplay
failing to show any discontent -a passive attempt
of finding yourself, leaning against a bookshelf
on top of the desk, your mind set on of burlesque.

Some red marks on a white collar,
a random thought of being bipolar
and everything goes back to normal;
it takes less than two seconds to zip (up),
smile to a stranger and become formal.

PARADISE BOUGHT

Who would have guessed,
that here in Paradis City,
all I can feel is self-pity?

Each wave brings more anger,
each word sounds stronger-
leaving seems more tempting.

Should I follow my instinct?
who should I call?
REALITY CALLS!
it`s only me again.

I`m walking on black clouds:
first step makes me feel dizzy,
the second fills my veins with blood,
my head is spinning fast while
my eyes are staring at the window.

84

An older demon surfaced,
with him, a grief I thought forgotten.
I know too well these symptoms,
and there is no happy ending.

"*Who are you?*"
My chest is burning,
breathing is hurting,
heart is aching.

Getting bored of riding these waves,
as much as I enjoy surfing the top,
I hate finding myself on the riverbed.

PINK

We paint everything in pink,
let's take a minute and think!
why? why do we do such a thing?
ignoring what the future may bring,
denying all could be gone within a blink.
Who pulls the strings?

Pink never reveals its true nature;
pink has a plethora of shades
depicting an emotional adventure
always surprising with its raids.

Pink was never my type or my pigment
I always preferred green: grass, trees, moss,
jade, caterpillars, frogs, Volts and windmills
instead of envy and Benjamin bills.

PREDICTION

A gypsy once said:
"Stay away from the water,
It will lead to your death!
Soon you'll be out of breath!"

She raised the left eyebrow
"Where there's love, there's sorrow"
"Listen well, girl", puffed slowly her claro,
"There might be no tomorrow!"

How was she able to see
what laid in front of me?
How did she foresee
who was my enemy?

Lack of inspiration
or divine intervention?

Nothing better to say
except my future was grey?

I mocked her prediction
considered it all fiction,
never been superstitious
maybe a bit malicious.

Amused and a 'lil scared
I was the one who dared
to ignore the foretelling
and smile while rebelling.

PERPETUAL TRAVELLER

Downtown or by the country side
that`s where I bide and glide:
no job, big plans, few bucks;
I pleaded my cause,
I played my hand.

Throughout my life
I drew many white fences,
packed and unpacked suitcases
without ever caring where to,
as long as I was with you.

Year after year, we followed
new trails, fell and wallowed
in the sand just to gain strength.

Constantly adjusting my focal length,
I gazed through the camera's lens,
flipping from bus to beetle and then benz
settling for more or less, according to the dress.

A new playground or couple of months
until I realized you were actually me,
the perpetual traveller.

RED PORTO GETAWAY

There's a thin line between this glass and privacy,
by the end of it I'm loosing my decency...
seems like fears and shame fade with this chalice,
an explosive attempt of regaining control
is taking over my body-
it must have gone straight to my head.

This time I'm chasing my dream;
you better tie me down cause I'm ready to go,
you better hold me down cause
I'm having my wings back.

Hold me down cause I will fly away,
tell me sweet little lies and then let me go,
fly away with my dream and find myself again.
Are you sure you want me to stay
this bottle is empty and no money to pay...

SHADOWS OF THE PAST

I see everywhere faces I once knew,
I see them in people I never met,
the resemblance is astonishing!

I recon smiles and grimes,
gestures and words I pick up passing by.
Makes me wonder which one is a better version?

The floaters I see are more than floaters,
within these glimmering specks of light, there's life.
I feel its warmth within this sea of souls.

Could we all come from the same mold?
Or it`s just a déjà-vu?

SHERLOCK'S CASE

There's no mystery I wouldn't solve,
always feared me being bold.
      Try me!

There`s no question I wouldn't`t answer
about the t(r)opic of Cancer.
      Ask me!

There's no place I wouldn't go,
carried away by the wind's last blow.
      Call me!

There`s no page I wouldn't read
just to see the way you lead!
      Inspire me!

There`s no dare I wouldn't take
to keep you longer awake!
     Love me!

There`s no song I wouldn't sing
for this precious living thing.
     Hear me!

There`s no thing I wouldn't do
let me walk you through...
     Trust me!

There's no doubt you would say "Yes"
we all saw it in the press!
     Fear me!

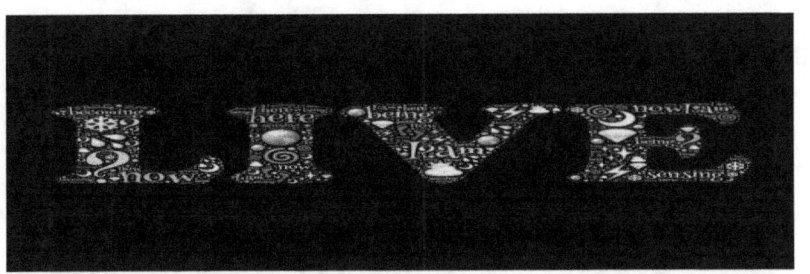

SHORT SUMMER POEM

I felt my wings again, I heard them fluttering,
inner warmth boosted up the confidence.
Gave up the plan of certainty
it was challenging my insanity,
all is vanity.
The only certain thing I know is that we die!
With summer, my soul awakes, I come alive;
only one sparkle is enough to start the engine.
Where to? it's time to set the course!
Not long ago Black paid us a visit,
rebalanced all beliefs,
weakened all the strengths.
I feared it less this time,
I live and love,
and then
I die.

SINS OF MEN

Life taste good when you`re in love,
never pick up a woman`s glove!
Can`t remember how it feels
being always meals on wheels?

Marriage`s never what you`d expect,
trouble starts with no respect;
up to you to do the Math
if it`s worth taking the mud bath.

Women always have a say
"poor guy, he`d better obey!";
even righteous crawls and tumbles
with parents` help, all crumbles.

SMOKE ROLLS

Light up your cigarette,
bring on the rum,
pour me a glass
and let's get drunk!
As the time stops,
and eyes get weary
hours are dilating,
you're flying on a tricycle.
The smoke rolls open your mind
to new unknown perspectives;
you're trying to capture
within a few words
the secrets of
a lost life.

What is the point of asking
questions without answers
or thinking of what ifs?
Rejoice you got the chance
to witness true love,
even if it lasted
no longer than
a kiss.

THE DREAM

First time I saw my daughter's face was in a dream
I still remember it, even it was for a glance -
she whispered something I couldn't understand
as if the words were spoken in a foreign language.

Her tiny little face, her big brown eyes,
the curls running on her face and neck,
the perfect folds of her little red dress
are embedded in my mind forever.

I woke up with cold tears on my face
and my heart aching, longing to touch
and hold her one more time; although
I knew that was not even possible.

The past and present are sipping on my couch
slouching without any sense of direction,
as if the time stopped and everything is floating,
how can I escape the world and get back to my
dream?

THE DOORS

Close those doors leading you to nowhere
your clenched fists, screams, anger roars,
yells or cries -everything must stop there,
even those ifs and deep hopes for being elsewhere...

Let it all go and make space for (self) love,
take an easier, smoother path,
don't tarnish or darken your heart
for whispered promises made under an alcove,
they ain't real, ain't going to be
breath them out, set yourself free.

It's time to move on, stop lingering on
whatever was, dwells in the past,
learn to keep your head straight,
learn to forgive and walk fast,

learn to have some faith,
if you can't swim,
go with the flow...

Better keep those doors locked,
no matter what they brought,
no matter what or how you fought:
sadness, tears or blissful laughs;
it's all done -it's all gone,
it lives within your mind,
it feeds upon your soul,
move on!

THE REASON WHY
(THE REVELATION)

From all the loves I had, felt and left behind
there's one I cherished more.
I asked myself why it burnt
within my soul for so long,
until one day the truth unfolded,
it all made sense within seconds:
those big brown eyes,
the wavy hair, the soft voice-
it all wore a familiar fatherly label!
Despite the fact they took different stands,
both preached the same thing: God and Love...
no wonder it burnt for so long...
that's what I call a revelation!

THE RIBBONS

Why can't I explain what is it that makes me cry,
when I think of you, my heart aches,
the thought of you brings back memories
of a little girl, feeling shunned
without even realizing when or why
or how that happened...
when did we loose that beautiful connection?
The ribbons are still here!

I skip a heart beat while listening to Bach
or opera and tears are running down my face,
the little girl shared your passion
tried her best to please or make you proud
she tried ballet, violin with no luck...
You were and still are her Sun!

TIME TO HIT THE ROAD

It's been a while since I got stuck in the city.
I got tired of the daily routine and endless demands.
I lost the notion of time trying to make my way
in the white shirts' world where nothing ever counts.

Today I made up my mind: I change my path
and leave behind all of my pains and plans.
My only mission is to hit the road and roam,
roam freely until I'd learnt the last drop of
knowledge put on my path,
until my tears lost their bitterness
and my eyes regained their playfulness.

UNFAIR

I checked my message box a thousand times
hoping that I would hear one word from you.
What are we waiting for I can't understand;
we stated the facts, made the addition
 still one plus one does not equal two,
cause I am still walking alone barefoot
while you're thousands of miles away.
Missing you wasn't supposed
 to feel this way...
Unfair!

It's unfair to see the rules of this game changing...
it's hard to keep up, how can I explain it to my heart
that your eyes are too weary to make a phone call
or write me a line from across the world?

I let you set the pace, it looks we stumbled, got stuck;
no news form you... What's going on? Be honest!
We fell from incendiary forbidden love into deafening
silence... Tell me, have you found someone else?
Don't be polite!

UTOPIA

Who plays by the rules, will always lose!
That day when there will be no money,
is so far far away, honey!
For now, we have rules and conditions,
that only fools obey.
No matter as much you try,
how good you are,
if you have no P.R.
You strive to keep up the pace,
even when you feel out of place,
you preach equity, cultural awareness,
where there's no fairness,
you can stack up degrees and diplomas,
you can forget you speak couple of idiomas,
none of this counts for those with big accounts;
you find yourself among big fish and sharks.

WENT BACK IN TIME

One suitcase traveled over the ocean,
carried some old forgotten memories
of faces and voices,
of youth and choices,
of promises and dreams,
of Sundays with ice creams.
All went upstream,
ended up, hanging on a beam!

Blown in the summer breeze,
my childhood pals left overseas,
immigrated as the flees.
No one left here? Jeez!

Where are the 9 red bricks
we used to play when the old
teacher called us pricks?

Those days, time had a different notion,
everything comes back in slow motion;
I fear the effect of this potion-
could it be the same balsamic lotion?
I grew up and forged myself,
I even passed the DELF!

Nowadays, it`s all Facebook:
the shared wall is just a hook,
keeps u posted on the turn I took,
all you have to do is look!

Packed in a hurry, a yellow envelope,
hides over thirty pictures,
small glimpses of my hero`s life,
most of them in the cathedral: his pride!

There he spent more than one decade
served the Almighty, and prayed,
twice was even on the blade
for refusing the red cold aid.

111

WHEN HEART DECIDES

With both hands tied
I continued my ride;
nothing else mattered
emotions, all scattered.

Almost ten years later,
encountered the Creator,
thought all was done...
when it had just begun.

Life seemed to short, unfair,
we weren't prepared
to leave it behind...
The truth: we were blind!

I opened each drawer,
went down to the core,
dusted off memories
remembered old enemies.

This carousel unraveled
the reason I traveled,
incognito, seeking new ways,
hoping for better days.

It`s hard to divide
ego from pride
when heart decides
who stays or dies.

WHEN YOU HERX

All my life I've been around pricks
and it's hard to believe or imagine
any of them would stick around
the moment I'd fall, cry or herx.

There's no lover when you're sick,
they're all worried you might prick,
hitting the "*fly*" mode as soon as you sneeze,
fearing that they'd have to be there
when you're down on your knees.

WILD CHILD

I wanted to tell you to look in the mirror,
this boy is not the one I fell for -
me, I haven't seen him for a while...
I fear you might have left him behind,
all caught up between your issues and fears.

Is it too late to bring him back while we're still young,
before we reach the point where we draw the line?

Last time I checked, he used to care,
plenty of things he questioned and dared,
he wasn't ashamed to walk hand in hand.

I miss those times when he used to say
"Good night, see you in the light!"
Oh God, how I miss that wild child!

VERTIGO (NON-SENSE)

I open one eye and it seems so far away,
I open both and still seems hard to reach,
I am going in circles...
Where is the fun?
No more candid moments from now on?

Once you knew it, there's not much to expect from it?
The top, the bottom, are they the same?
Shouldn't be a difference in between?
 I climb over and over again,
I can`t stop asking if all this is just a pattern
or maybe a mice race?

VOICELESS

Today I talked to you, but you are not the person
I once knew; your face kept the same features -
some wrinkles and white hair in your moustache,
the same smile and cologne waking up my senses.
I talked to you but you seemed to be a distant version
of the man I needed; seeing you're somehow absent,
I resumed to daily simple topics and let you be,
but inside me, I felt the pain was bubbling up..

118

It's understandable you had your share of worries
and troubles, personal pursuits, interests;
old age made you turn a blind eye on the world,
focused on your old system of beliefs.

Although I grew up, deep down inside,
I'm still that little girl who needs your love...
because of the love I have for you,
my fears and emotions leave me voiceless.

YOU KNOW IT ALL!

You sound so smart and you use big words,
you talk about the world being at crossroads.

You went beyond the common daily quest of wisdom
while most of us plunge in a delightful boredom.

You say you want to bring everyone up
cause life on Earth can't be so fucked up!

You dream to get humanity out of its knees
but how do you imagine doing this?

You're sure being really up for this task
it's not about you wearing a *know it all* mask?

You look annoyed and bored by simplest questions;
how can it be that you're not even open for
suggestions?

When challenged, the tone of your voice
gets a higher pitch; therefore, my friend,
take a step back and check if there's a glitch!

You doubt reason and expertise with no proof but
your word; anything one'd say, takes you from
question to a verbal sword.

You can't expect people to believe and take your word
for granted when you expose condescension;
is this what you intended?

Relying solely on your knowledge with no demos, tact
or facts won't help you reach or change the human
mindset. No impact!

YOUR LAST DAY

Remember what we promised the first night together!
Scold me, fight me, but please don't let me go;
spill out the venom, open your heart
talk to me like as if it's your last day!

Remember the soul can be fed with silent dreams,
it can be healed with foggy thoughts and cries;
we agreed to be here and stay, so please
talk to me as if it's your last day!

Remember how much we liked to fly and dance,
lose ourselves in the ocean of sounds,
intoxicated with love and letters,
talk to me as if it's your last day!

The End

NOTE FROM LAVI PICU

Thank you for reading BURDEN OF LOVE.

I hope you enjoyed reading it. If you liked it, please take a moment and leave a short review at your favourite online retailer, on Amazon or add it to your GoodReads list.

I welcome contact with readers. Check out my author page on Facebook in order to have a sneak peak into my latest projects or drop me a comment. I'd love to hear your thoughts.

EDITORIAL REVIEW

"Lavi Picu, takes you with her again, through all burden of love. She calls upon the ancient Gods of love. You tumble, you stumble, you fall and you rise, you long for love and you run from love. You are led and you are misled, yet you wish to be a word in all tumbling and stumbling of falling in love and falling from love."

Dana Caban_ The Shame